Driving Into the Dark

Jeremy Gadd

Driving Into the Dark

Driving Into the Dark
ISBN 978 1 76109 407 1
Copyright © text Jeremy Gadd 2022
Cover image: Kayle Kaupanger from Unsplash

First published 2022 by
Ginninderra Press
PO Box 3461 Port Adelaide 5015
www.ginninderrapress.com.au

Contents

What is the Point	7
This is a Poem	8
The Boy Who Killed an Owl	9
What is Commonly Called	14
For Harry	15
The Green-tiled Bathroom	16
Come the Comet	17
A State Funeral Remembered	19
Greek Tragedy	21
HMS Repulse & HMS Prince of Wales	23
Invictus Sydney 2018	24
For 'The Few'	26
Baby Boomer Blues	27
It is Christmas	28
The Missing Biscuits	30
Many Believe	31
To All	32
Deep Are the Dungeons	33
Notre Dame de Paris	34
Love 1635	35
My Neighbour	36
Trust	37
The Memorial Service	38
As We Get Older	39
Lower Fort Street	40
Fake News	41
Are We the Last?	42
Mysterious Mistra	43
I Sometimes Wake	45
When My Father Died	46

Shadows Long	47
November Lilies	48
Dylan's Dad	49
If You Live Long Enough	50
Sunset Ferry	51
A New Guard	52
The Wind	53
Inanna and the Gatekeeper	54
When Southerly Gales Blow	58
The Great Divide	59
Drought	60
Love	61
In a time	62
Covid-19	63
Angelic Beauty	64
We Were	65
Portals	66
The Cadaver on the Couch	68
Only Love	69
For My Brother	70
Ozymandias Revisited	71
Ever Wondered	72
The Twisted Ladder	73
Charlotte Corday	75
Lock Down	76
To an Aborted Child	77
The Temple	78
Squalls	79
I Met a Man	80
Stay a While	81
Acknowledgements	82

What is the Point

What is the point of studying a language,
its grammar and its verse forms, of immersing
oneself in its literary traditions, when the
cultural identity it represents is being
constantly undermined by elements opposed
to its existence? If a culture is the collective
ideas, customs and social behaviour of a particular
people or society, what is the point of trying
to perpetuate a tradition when the shared values
it represents are deliberately being eroded?
The point is that cultures are continuing constructions,
requiring constant nurturing to survive and,
if they don't receive it, they fall. Knowing this,
I metaphorically scratch this graffito on Time's wall.

This is a Poem

This is a poem for the poor,
huddled, hands outstretched,
outside the door.
This is a requiem for life
filled with wonder and with strife.
This is song for all the sinners –
more than many have had hot dinners.
This is in praise of all the seeds
that will, one day, grow into great deeds.
This is a re-call for poison pens,
to be, anonymously, returned,
not spurned, before being
crushed and burned.
This is a fervent prayer
for the ill, their cross to bear.
This is a problematic paean –
long, short, short, short –
to those caught stealing
from those who bought and
those seeking signs or healing
from toxic lead-painted ceilings.
This is all poets have to give,
for no one has long to live.

The Boy Who Killed an Owl

As if dealt dark cards or the Joker
when playing Old Maid, what began
as a game got out of hand and
brought shame that scarred
him for life. It began after school
when, looking for fun, some bare-
kneed, primary-aged boys, threaded,
single file, through the trees,
pretending to be mighty hunters.
They carried sticks for spears and,
being young, few fears and even less
respect for the fauna around them.

They came across a big bird,
motionless, hunched on a low bough
but the boys did not know they'd met
an owl. The bird sensed the boys and
tilted its large head towards them.
Blinking slowly, it watched their
approach with saucer-like eyes
before hooting to warn of its presence.

But little boys can be wicked and,
thinking to scare and goad it to fly,
they egged each other on until,
the boy bringing up the rear, hurled
his stick – the first stone – and
by mischance, misfortune or destiny,
it forcefully struck and disembowelled
the unfortunate, inoffensive owl!
The bird fell, fluttering, to the ground.

Comprehending he had killed;
that he had taken life, the boy
could barely breath beneath
the weight of his responsibility.
The shock chilled him and, horrified
by the dead bird before him, he
wished the deed undone – too late.
The boys buried the bird and, uneasy,
swore to tell no one before, furtively,
creeping from the tainted place…
At home, the now troubled boy
looked up the bird's characteristic
features in his parents' book of birds
and learned it was an owl and,
from further reading, that owls
– like all wildlife – are special.

He learnt the owl is a symbol of wisdom;
that the ancient Athenians chose
the image of an owl to adorn their
currency and represent their god,
Athena, guardian of the Acropolis:
that, as owls are nocturnal, they
are often associated with mysticism,
the dark and the dead; the
supernatural spirits of the night;
that some believe a hooting owl
means someone is going to die.
And the boy who killed the owl
began to die of shame. There
was no excuse for a deed so foul.

From that time, he changed
from being gregarious and wild
to a more introspective child.
The boy remained in his room,
avoiding the friends who had
been with him and, to his parents'
consternation, became withdrawn.
At senior school, his interest
in studying markedly waned.
Somehow he scraped a pass.

The years passed too, and the boy
who killed an owl became a man
but, no use, the remorse remained
and the dead bird's demise continued
to haunt him. He left home and
held several unsatisfactory jobs.
Once, on the threshold of what
might have become a career,
the owl loomed in his memory
and he lost confidence in his
capabilities and withdrew his application.
He fell in love and was on the
verge of asking to marry but,
at the moment he was about to
propose, the owl materialised –
a grisly apparition –over her shoulder
and feelings of unworthiness
became overwhelming and he
walked away from the relationship.

The older he got, the more he saw
himself as the boy who killed an owl,
until, eventually, he was unemployable.
Destitute, he became a recluse,
begging money for beer and sleeping
in fear on the street and in public parks.

Vagabonds become used to abuse,
being treated disdainfully, picked on
for fights and, in his psychologically
cowed plight, his hair turned white.
He was ready to throw in the towel
when, one day, he found a lame lark,
singing joyfully despite its injury.
He tried to ignore it but it insistently
sang until he was captivated by
the life force it emanated.
He gently made a splint for the
bird's broken bone and fed it
until well enough to fly home and
something stirred in his empty heart.

He looked for work and found it
as a part-time repairman and,
with his hard-earned wages,
re-built a caravan to live in – and,
for the remainder of his allotted span,
cared for hurt and hungry birds.

People brought him sick pets
and, even vets, left recuperating birds
in his healing care until, although
threadbare, he became a valued
contributor to his community. But,
best of all, he found the boy inside
him, the boy who killed an owl
had gone and, despite continuing,
though subdued, residual guilt –
still present like a fading stain –
he felt he had atoned and could
finally live with himself again.

What is Commonly Called

What is commonly called a weed
has pushed, wriggled and writhed
through a fissure in the concrete pavement,
seeking sunshine, photosynthesis, survival.
The tendril is weak, fragile, vulnerable,
its very being tenuous but, that stem
extruding from where its seed was blown,
accidentally washed or lodged,
proclaims nature will one day reclaim its own.
Its roots will create cracks that, in turn,
will receive other migrant seeds or spores.
Organisms that will grow and expand,
crumbling the concrete around it into sand.

For Harry

The child asks, eyes wide as pies,
whether I'll be able to be by his
side after my inevitable demise?
But how to respond to a loved grandson
without endangering his sense of fun?
If you aspire to play World Cup soccer
or to become a rock and roll star,
I'll be the lucky bounce of the ball
or a memorable riff on your guitar.
If you want to attain athletic fame
and are sprinting to catch a competitor
before the end of a measured track,
I'll be that breath of wind you feel
pushing you along at your back.

The Green-tiled Bathroom

A lifetime later, images of the green-tiled bathroom
still recur – like an awful film noir segment – in her mind,
a kraken repeatedly rearing out of the dark,

deep, abyssal trench of repressed memories.
She can recall the colour and texture of the tiles,
their symmetry and the shade of the grout that defined them,

the details on which she concentrated in her attempt to
disassociate from what was being done.
The family home's green-tiled bathroom was, to her,

a room of horror, no less awful than a dungeon of depravity.
The green-tiled bathroom was where she paid the piper;
the fee for child-minding that left her with a lifetime of purgatory.

Come the Comet

Ten millennia ago, before philosophies like 'existentialism' and
definitions, such as 'prehistoric' and 'neolithic', people built Gobekli
Tepe's temples and, on its so-called 'vulture' column,
symbolically predicted the return of a cosmic storm.

Come the comet,
the minutiae of modern
life will be meaningless.
Come the comet,
who will care what label they wear;
about the demise of the polar bear.
Come the comet,
as we wait for the world to shatter,
identity will cease to matter;
ditto whether life is tough or
presented on a silver platter.
Come the comet,
international disputes and
being of high repute will
become inconsequential.
Come the comet
and its accompanying
global cataclysm,
race relations will take
back seat as home and
high-rise melt in the heat.
Come the comet,
will Earth's axis tilt?
Will the magnetic poles reverse,
triggering tectonic shift or, worse,
allow in harmful solar radiation?

Come the comet,
incinerated forests and
other ubiquitous natural
mass destruction will render
nuclear weapons superfluous.
Come the comet,
those concerned with climate
change and environmental
preservation will seem deranged.

Come the comet,
will anyone care about religion?
Will Allah save the world from oblivion?
Will Paradise have enough virgins
for the millions of Moslem martyrs?
Come the comet,
Will the Christian dead arise and
ghoulishly queue for judgement
where St Michael waits?
And, after the comet,
if the calamity abates
and some survive and,
as at Gobekli Tepe,
seek to build a new society,
to reinvent their world and
attempt to give sense
to a violent and mostly
incomprehensible universe,
pray they ameliorate the
human propensity to divide
and differentiate…

A State Funeral Remembered

A recent spate of biographical
movies reminded me of a state funeral
watched, in flickering black and white,
and relayed by, then, technologically
innovative satellite, from frozen London,
beset with wintery gales,
to hot and dusty rural New South Wales
and, although young, I was well aware –
as when seeing Turner's depiction
of *The Fighting Temeraire* – that
I was viewing the end of an era:
Britain was burying Winston Churchill.
But it isn't the pageantry I recall:
the artillery salute reverberating
in the still, frigid air or the slow,
measured tread of the sailors,
leaning and swaying on the ropes
in unison as they hauled the gun carriage
up Ludgate Hill's slope to St Paul's,
packed with sombre dignitaries;
or Queen Elizabeth breaking convention
to receive the commoner's flag draped coffin;
or Menzies' eulogy from the crypt,
lauding how Churchill lit 'lamps of hope';
or Handel's *Death March*;
the bugler's call to reveille;
the RAF flying past in his honour or
the cranes lowered along the Thames.

I remember most the coffin's journey,
by train, to Bladon's country cemetery,
and the ordinary citizens who lined the route,
waiting to pay homage: the bemedalled men
who stood at attention in ill-fitting uniforms;
the man wearing a dented metal helmet
saluting from a roof; passers-by
who simply stopped and removed
hats or bowed their heads in respect;
the dignified elderly woman, wrapped
in coat and scarf against the cold,
holding aloft a sign which read,
'Thank you and goodbye.'

Greek Tragedy

'Novelist George Johnston was married to writer Charmian Clift
and was the father of two sons, Jason and the poet Martin Johnston,
and two daughters, Gae & Shane.'

Your name, 'Shane', at the end of your father's
biographical note; briefly referenced for posterity.
Is that all that is left of a life?
You were more than that, much more to me…

These black and white photographs capture
mother, daughter, brother Martin, hand in hand,
strolling along Hydra's coarse beach sand – but photos
are one-dimensional and do not do justice

to the innocence and vigour of childhood or to
that idyllic time when your parents shared creative synergy.
You were part of a unique, expatriate literary community.
You listened to Leonard Cohen's lyrics and to him

practising guitar long before he became an iconic star.
Did anything indicate Cohen might eclipse Johnston
and/or predict your family's tragedies to come?
You were flesh and blood, full of fun, politically aware,

with emotional empathy and fond of bathing
in the sun and – understandably – most things Greek.
My memory is of a young single mother
(when society scorned such entities)

without regular income (in the days before social security);
doting on your infant child but sleeping on a mattress
upon a rented floor; enjoying erudite company, even
tolerating the occasional bore, while holding your intellectual

own among raucous male camaraderie intent on beating
the closing bell at Balmain's bohemian Forth & Clyde Hotel
– featured in Sandy Harbutt's cult film *Stone* – simultaneously
concerned about baby and sitter back home (pre-mobile phone).

I recall you desperate for a dollar and
needing friends – but not of losing hope.
I lost touch and later learnt you did not cope,
that you had slid down a darkening slope.

You chose to walk to a different beat
and, like the soldiers who fell defending Crete,
will always remain young.
These images of you are bitter-sweet.

Your name, 'Shane', at the end of your father's
biographical note; briefly referenced for posterity.
Is that all that is left? You were
more than that, much more to me…

HMS Repulse & HMS Prince of Wales

They sailed to defend Singapore,
so Singaporeans might not
become slaves to the Rising Sun;
might continue to be merchants
enjoying the fruits of their trade;
but, now, both battleships,
vanquished by samurai blades,
lie many fathoms beneath the sea
but, apparently, not deep enough…
The rusted vessels are being raided,
dredged, broken up, degraded,
for prized, low-background,
pre-nuclear, scrap metal and
sailors' bones are being lost in
the slush of the seabed, tossed aside
or being crushed within the wrecked
hulls by those whose culture,
supposedly, venerates the deceased.
No respect, no homage, no honour
for these desecrated dead…

Invictus Sydney 2018

Peak hour commuters, standing
like vertically packed sardines
in the vestibule of the carriage,
surged to exit once it slid to
a standstill at Wynyard Station.
As the passengers dispersed,
he was revealed like an actor
when curtains part or when
a character is spotlighted
onstage. Bearded, burly but
with muscular, tattooed arms,
the insignia on his rucksack
and his soldierly bearing
betrayed his previous vocation.
If able to stand, he would
have towered above ordinary
mortals but, restricted to a
wheelchair, there were no limbs
where his legs should have been.

The last passenger alighted
and one swipe of the chair's
wheel rims with his palms
rolled him to the intercom.
'Ramp please,' he politely
requested the guard and,
as he tapped his fingers
impatiently and the entire train
waited for the guard to bring
the boarding ramp to enable
his chair to reach the platform,
I sensed his vexation was not
due to the delay but at his
having to rely on others –
and that his struggle to
retain his personal freedom
of movement was a metaphor
for national independence
and a reminder of the
cost and debt owed.

For 'The Few'

'From this day to the ending of the world,
But we in it shall be rememberèd –
We few, we happy few, we band of brothers;' – *Henry V*

James Edward Gadd,
Flight Sergeant, 611 Squadron,
is listed among the aircrew named
as having fought in the Battle of Britain.

Hard to imagine now: aircraft soaring;
the reek of oil and stench of rubber;
the cramped cockpit; the vibration
and roar from the Merlin engine;

the claustrophobic oxygen mask;
radio static and warnings of the
waiting Hun in the sun in his ear;
the taste of fear – of death – and worse –

of being maimed or burnt alive.
Did you survive? Were you aware
as you flew, you would become
known as one of 'The Few'?

(Churchill knew his Shakespeare.)
Were you aware your endurance,
resistance, resilience would be as
important, for the future of freedom,

as at Marathon, Thermopylae or Tours?
Or were you yet another young man,
future on hold, without a plan,
simply doing his duty?

Baby Boomer Blues

In the aftermath of Armageddon,
the ill-wedded allies begot a generation
which rejected militarism and, naively
assuming all shared similar values,
grew up believing in the nobility of humanity,
in tolerance, friendship and generosity,
in love, peace and happiness – not war –
and strove to make the world a better place.
And, for a moment, their hopes almost happened…
but, as they grew old in the genial and
self-indulgent West, blinkered in their opinions,
assumptions, attitudes and convictions,
they failed to notice the rest of
the world had not shared their beliefs.

It is Christmas

A wet night on an urban highway
and, without explanation,
traffic is at a standstill.

Hundreds of headlights
probe and grope into the dark
and drizzle like insect antennae

but nothing approaches from
the opposite direction.
Only time passes: minutes, an hour.

Some switch engines off;
others open car windows
as windscreens mist.

It is Christmas and appointments,
dinners, functions are being missed.
Some drivers are visibly irritable.

Dampness swathes the darkness,
envelopes glistening metal and,
like caterpillars, the columns of tailgating

vehicles begin to edge forward,
stop and proceed, slow,
stop and start again until,

finally, the car radio advises a young
woman crossing the road up ahead
has been hit by a vehicle running a red light.

The site of the incident is eventually reached:
traffic police cars, ambulances and a tent
erected on the road to shelter

the pedestrian and paramedics from
the rain as they fought to save her life;
the guilty vehicle with its tortured bonnet.

Next morning the news announces
the woman died in hospital overnight
and that blood tests confirmed

the driver was drunk. We were
late home but others
will miss more than Christmas.

The Missing Biscuits

It was in aisle three I panicked;
while looking for the crisp lemon biscuits;
your favourites! They weren't
where they should have been…
and it was only then the import
of your earlier call, 'possible stroke,
ambulance, intensive care…'
and a sudden sense of despair
and the thought that you, like the biscuits,
might not always be there – overwhelmed me.

Many Believe

Many believe the Middle East conflict
is perplexing, difficult, impenetrable,
a demanding diplomatic labyrinth
absorbing billions in inter-generational aid.
But it is actually easy to understand.
Ancient Zoroastrians believed two elemental
forces struggle for control of the cosmos;
right or wrong; truth or lie; light and dark
and that good deeds encouraged happiness
and kept anarchy and chaos at bay;
a fundamental choice for all.
'Thus spake Zarathustra': there is a
universal struggle between two creeds:
one celebrates death, the other life: *L'chaim!*

To All

To all the transitory clouds, flitting across the sky;
to all the losers looking up at them and wondering why;
to all the dispirited men, viewing life through an alcoholic haze;
to all the blowsy blondes yearning for better days.
To the poetry of motion, of Marilyn not Andrew,
to the poetry of immobility, the majesty of ocean;
to all the old and to the infirm, fighting to stay alive,
to all the drones, busy in the hive;
to all the young and vibrant, oblivious to the fact they'll die;
to all the happy swine, muddy in the sty.
To the aspirational, who are yet to learn their limits;
to all the Peacock-spiders, thanks for adding to our awe.
To all the lucky, whose confidence is yet to be pricked;
to all the vagaries of life, even to the ailment that gets you,
they are all part of the process – one day the sun sets without you.
To all the unlucky, whose boats are yet to find the shore,
to all the pilgrims, arriving where they began, footsore;
there are no words of wisdom, there's no blueprint for success;
take happiness where you find it and live…live…live

Deep Are the Dungeons

Deep are the dungeons of the dawn
where evil waits and spawns.
High are the heroes of the atmosphere
ballooning there, feigning fear.
Long are the lips of the parasites
lasciviously licking soaring kites.
In between are those seldom seen,
those who could or might have been.

Notre Dame de Paris

(for Fr Jean-Marc Fournier)

Outside, onlookers wept,
prayed, sang hymns while, inside,
beneath the waterfalls of flame,
the grey tears of molten lead
and charred and burning debris
falling from the fire ravaged
roof and collapsed wooden spire,
he stood – alone amidst the
carnage – having already organised
the rescue of religious relics
and aware Quasimodo's towers
and bells were in jeopardy,
the ex-army chaplain, who'd
given succour in Afghanistan
and to the Parisian fire brigade;
who gave collective absolution
during the massacre of innocents
at the Bataclan, used the saved
Blessed Sacrament to perform
a benediction: calling upon
his Saviour to save the beloved
Lady of Paris – and it still stands…

Love 1635

They hung him from a
gibbet, erected on a hill,
for the murder of poor
Thomas Heath and, as it was
during the seventeenth century,
in an inclement decision –
part of the judgement – his
punishment for his abhorrent
sin included letting his lifeless
body swing, pecked by birds
and gnawed by rodents,
rotting in the rain and biting
wind until, what was left
of his remains, mummified.
And, whether robins chirped or
carrion crows cried, whether
gales blew or breezes sighed,
every twilight she came:
an elderly woman, usually
cloaked against the cold, she
would struggle up the knoll
and, kneeling below the
corpse's clawed feet, talk to it,
as if still alive, and, like a nun
or priest preparing to shrive,
pray for succour; for the
loss of her loved one, for
the murdered man and
for the soul of her only son.

My Neighbour

My neighbour feeds the magpies.
He thinks he is being kind
but, to the result, he is blind.
Warbling to greet the dawn,
the magpies queue from first light
and, rising late, he doesn't see
the birds are a blight – that while
he sleeps, the magpies strut
about on stalk-like legs,
and prey upon, peck and devour,
the rare and pretty blue wrens' eggs.

Trust

We have to trust the pilot of our plane,
that the driver next to us will stay in their lane,
that the politician with Armageddon's button is sane.
Trust encourages confidence,
offers security, reliability, stability,
optimism and certainty for the future.
Trust is necessary for long-term relationships –
within the corporate world, in religious faith
or intimate consanguinity.
A child's trust, substantiated, manifests in
physical and emotional safety; mistrust
to misgivings, suspicion, doubt and cynicism.
But do we trust until disproven or mistrust till proven sound?
Trust is often sought but seldom found.

The Memorial Service

For Ken Horler

She wore large, round sunglasses
and worked her way along the line of
mourners waiting for entry to the church,
as if a movie star mingling at a garden party.
Whether she was looking for friends,
ex-lovers or simply networking was hard to tell.
Always big she was a barrel now
and, with ample cleavage on show,
gave the appearance she had something to sell.
Well-known amongst her clique,
to her regret, this actress had
never become a house-hold name.
It was rumoured she had fallen on hard times,
even penury and, like Blanche, often
dependent on the kindness of friends
but, from her imperious approach,
her expensive apparel, the presence
of poverty was not apparent –
nor was any associated humility.
She slowly drew abreast and,
lifting her shades, peered at me
quizzically: I said my name and
she stared, disdainfully, before saying,
'Oh, yes' and, lowering her glasses,
moved on to the man behind me.

As We Get Older

As we get older, the measure of our pleasure
becomes, what was once, unimportant –
like uninterrupted sleep – and, reaching
the top of our towers of time; bent like peasants
beneath the weight of what we consider memorable;
only vanity, questions and recollections remain.
Do we still retain some of youth's vitality?
Will we leave the world better than when we came?
Living life has its fees but we are the sum of our memories.
There is also a natural kindness associated with ageing:
as gravity takes its toll and lines and wrinkles proliferate,
so eyesight simultaneously fails and extra follicles
and furrows remain blurred or unseen in our reflections.
Memories, similarly, become increasingly selective.

Lower Fort Street

Lower Fort Street took its name
from a fort once part of Kipling's Great Game.

The guns from the *Sirius* became a battery
and Lieutenant Dawes signal station inspired an observatory.

In the houses that line its once cobbled pavements
lived officers from the finest regiments

who'd fought campaigns in India against Tipoo,
at Bunker Hill and at Waterloo.

Warehouses and hovels became heritage,
Billy Blue's ferry became a bridge.

Redeveloped after a break out of plague
memories since have become more than vague

but the Garrison Church (or Holy Trinity)
continues to remind residents of divinity.

Lower Fort Street has seen it all,
an empire came – and did fall –

while the Gadigal picked over the foreshore nearby
admiring the vastness of the enduring blue sky.

Gadigal: local Indigenous tribe

Fake News

Marcellus opined, 'There are more things in Heaven
and Earth, Horatio, than are dreamt of in your philosophy…'
So how do we interpret Piri Reis' map?
And what about the Vimana, flying flower
carriages, in the Vedic Raymayana?
Is reality really a reflection on the wall of
Plato's cave and do the ruins of Atlantis
actually exist deep beneath the ocean waves?
What if the millennial mist surrounding the Sumerian
King's List and Gobleki Tepe's apparent age –
supposedly from the last ice age – is true?
Is it all a conspiracy and are we puppets of the Illuminati?
Should we simply accept what we are told
or test, verify or deny what we are being sold?

Are We the Last?

Is the current generation of Homo Sapiens –
from the Latin, 'Wise Man' – the last?
Are the existing members of humanity
like Neanderthals and Denisovans,
now facing extinction? Will gene-editing
technology, bionic engineering, enhanced
resistance to disease and a subsequent
increase in life expectancy lead to
exploitation by the mega-rich who –
in the process of redesigning themselves
and their children – create an underclass
of unimproved humans, drones to drive the hive.
Will these super humans of the future even
remember the fragility of being human?

Mysterious Mistra

Mysterious Mistra, high on the mountain,
known as the wonder of Morea,
where medieval artists and architects
mingled by fountains in the shadows
of the ruins of the Norman fortress
or walked and wandered among pines,
Cyprus, gnarled, venerable, olive
trees, accompanied by belled sheep;
where worshippers prayed in
churches graced with fine frescoes,
or inhaled cool, clean air while
absorbing spectacular views
from the balconies of aristocratic
palaces and monasteries – where
Gemistus Pletho once sat in his
library replete with rare copies of
archaic Hellenic authors, including
Plato and Plotinus, contemplating
a perfect universe, without beginning
or end in time and, being perfect,
believing nothing could make it better.
Pletho rejected Christianity and
dogma about a brief life of evil
followed by perpetual happiness
and hoped for a return to pagan gods.

Pletho believed in karma; that the
human soul is reincarnated
and that a divine order governs
the organisation of bees,
the foresight of ants, the dexterity
of spiders, the growth of plants,
magnetism and alchemy.
Ezra Pound, in his cage, was
intrigued by Pletho and his
Cantos mention how Pletho
met Cosimo de Medici in
Florence and how Cosimo
financed the Accademia Platonica,
which translated Plato into
Latin and reintroduced Neoplatonist
texts to a later age.

    And, in doing so,
Pletho and Cosimo fulfilled their
divine destinies. For divine isn't
necessarily a grand gesture or saintly
accomplishment. Akin to butterflies
flapping their wings, they gave impetus
to a ripple that became a tsunami
as the Renaissance enveloped Europe.
Like conversations about Michelangelo,
cultures come and cultures go.

I Sometimes Wake

I sometimes wake and feel my soul is scattered,
shattered, blown or eroded by photon winds
to the farthest reaches of the universe,
to black voids of unimaginable emptiness,
to shadowy, negative, emotional plasmic
membranes within other peoples' minds;
to other dimensions physics can describe
but which I cannot begin to visualise and,
feeling the need to summon and retrieve
my confused and disjointed psyche,
I then begin the onerous rehabilitation,
the painstaking re-construction of my gestalt –
that which makes me more than the sum of my parts.
On most occasions, however, a coffee will suffice.

When My Father Died

When my father died, my mother,
in her grief, chose to believe he
had become a certain, blinking, star;
a sentinel eye in the night sky.
She would often turn off her television
and sit, contented, in her belief
he devotedly watched over her.
I once encountered her conversing,
smiling rapturously, alone.
If her delusion brought comfort in her
bereavement, who was I to try to
debate the secular and supernatural?
Provided a belief system is harmless
to others, does it need to be rational?

Shadows Long

Shadows long and shadows short,
dance, writhe or consort on the walls of Plato's cave.
Shadows do not own their shape;
but rely on that of their origin –
whether alive or inanimate stone –
a shadow cannot survive alone.
As with the shadow persona of the mind:
lifting a roller-blind lets light in; so,
assimilating the shadow brings insight.
For the shadow is our unchosen choice –
that which we choose not to be, that which we,
consciously, refuse voice; and, whether
a voice of depravity or replete with creativity,
listening to both nurtures a healthy psyche.

November Lilies

November lilies were nodding in the breeze
like casual acquaintances passing when
a friend called to say a mutual friend had died.
Did I want to know the details of her death?
And I thought, we die in increments; by gasps
or by sudden demise and death is definitive
but I would rather know more about how she lived,
her idiosyncrasies; her irrepressible *joie de vivre,*
for it is the living entity who will always occupy my heart,
and death will find us impossible to part.
We humans are individually distinctive, unique:
sometimes attractive in body and mind
and sometimes not or unkind but, even after
mortality, there is only human interconnectivity.

Dylan's Dad

Dylan Thomas' learned but distant dad,
was an aspirant poet and performer who,
to his dismay, made his living each day
teaching English to Welsh schoolchildren.
They say some do while others teach and,
as DJ's chubby child would never play rugby
for Wales, he instilled in him his own
love of literature and language and,
like a stage mother, lived vicariously through his son,
constantly encouraging, critiquing and amending
the results of his nascent craft and,
as the child endlessly strived to please
his remote but admired father, he lived
to see the boy become what he always wanted to be.

If You Live Long Enough

If you live long enough, you will find
the world in which you came of age
redefined by younger generations,
resulting in elation or frustration.
All will change or be redefined, including –
to the disturbance of your comfort zone –
societal values, thought set in stone.
What was *de rigueur* will be denigrated;
what was once unreservedly accepted
questioned, undermined or redesigned.
Those you respected might be disgraced;
those who were nowhere might achieve first
place and even the heroes you once adored
become objects of ridicule or abhorred.

Sunset Ferry

I took a sunset Sydney ferry:
it left the Quay punctually
as the Bridge and surrounding
city high-rise, including Harry
Seidler's ugly Blues Point tower,
turned to dark silhouettes,
starkly outlined against a sky
suffused with residual orange hues.

Black water lapped against the hull
and the throb of engines resonated
inside tired passengers' skulls and,
as the ferry tilted a degree as it
turned toward the open sea,
enigmatic clouds appeared to
follow, as if in empathy. And,
as day continued further west,
the ferry carried me into the
Prussian blue of approaching
night – and rest…

A New Guard

A new praetorian guard now determines the
policies of media-driven western democracies
and who becomes prime minister or president.
These modern centurions wield weapons more
insidious than mere sharpened steel; their barbs are
poisoned and tipped with bile while artifice, spin and
guile disguise the motives of their biased spiels.
They are the commentators, editors, executive producers,
whose articles, editorials and programs conspire
to seduce and induce constituents to concur with
the wishes of their magnates – while the public believes
they impartially act in the community's best interest.
Instead, they impose their unelected will
on those who bear the brunt of parliament's bills.

The Wind

The wind bends trees to its will
like a dominatrix preparing a
submissive for punishment;
forcefully rattles the locked door,
a stranger demanding admittance.
The wind spies at the keyhole,
breathing heavily as it tries to wriggle
between the skirting boards and floor
and then scurries on to vibrate windows.
The wind is a dubious character lurking outside,
barred from entry, envious of the comfort inside.

Inanna and the Gatekeeper

Finally responding to her sister's
anguish and anger, the Goddess
decided to descend but – at the entrance
to the underworld – a Gatekeeper
appeared and blocked the Goddess's path.
'I have come to see my older sister,'
the Goddess, Inanna, informed him.
Sometimes known as Neti, the Gate-
keeper's features were Neanderthal.
He appraised her and nodded but insisted,
'Those who descend must disrobe.'

Inanna initially hesitated but then
removed her hat, shaped like an
eight-pointed star, and offered it to
the Gatekeeper. He looked at the hat
in disdain before taking and crushing
it in one huge hand. The Gatekeeper
remained motionless and said nothing,
as if expecting more, so Inanna took
off her celestial blue lapis lazuli earrings
and also gave them to the Gatekeeper.
'You may pass,' he said, and Inanna
walked down an inclining corridor
until she came to a second gate.
Although she thought him behind her,
the same Gatekeeper emerged to challenge her.
'Those who descend must disrobe,' he repeated.

Inanna removed the threaded pearls
she wore around her neck and which rose
and rested upon her pale breasts as she breathed.
The Gatekeeper accepted the pearls and,
admiring their lustre, rolled them between
his fingers as if fondling her nipples.
Inanna's complexion flushed but he
eventually said 'Pass,' and she walked
until she came to another gate.
The same Gatekeeper appeared before her.
'Those who descend must disrobe'

Inanna stared at him but obeyed.
She removed her cloak woven with
dove feathers and edged with priceless
fine filigree and undid her gold breastplate
and passed both to the Gatekeeper.
He felt the feathered cloak with his hands
and stared at the metal work before
grinning and grunting, 'Pass.' But
Inanna was soon confronted by another gate
and the same Gatekeeper, who again said,
'Those who descend must disrobe.'

Inanna removed the girdle that clung to her hips,
reputedly made by worms from the east,
her gown of identity, and tossed it at his feet.
It fell lightly like gossamer on still dawn air.
The Gatekeeper collected the garment and ran
the expensive fabric between his dirty fingers
before, smiling sardonically, ushering her
to a fifth gate – where he emerged yet again.
'Those who descend must disrobe.'

This time Inanna undid the clasps that
secured her robe to her shoulders. She
let it fall to the ground and stepped forward.
Standing in her underdress, like a poor person
in a single garment, she left the dress on the
ground for the Gatekeeper to pick up
before advancing to yet another gate.
Came the now familiar instruction:
'Those who descend must disrobe.'

Inanna raised her arms and,
lifting the underdress over her head,
stood before the Gatekeeper in her
bosom bandage and a breech-cloth
that hid her thighs and sex.
Inanna untied the bosom bandage and
stood proudly before the Gatekeeper.
The Gatekeeper said, 'Pass' and licked
his lips lasciviously as she passed in
a perfumed mist and advanced to the seventh gate.
'Those who descend must disrobe.'

Inanna only had one piece of wardrobe to
remove, and she stood nude before the
Gatekeeper, resplendent in her beauty.
The Gatekeeper's gaze roamed and slid
over her like slime but, instead of being
ashamed or timid, the Goddess seemed
to grow in stature, radiance and confidence.
Like a cat stretching, she extended her arms
and, almost flaunting, elegantly posed
with grace and allure, allowing the Gate-
keeper to luxuriate in her womanhood.

The Gatekeeper, suddenly uneasy
and afraid, said, 'You are meant to
be naked, demure and submissive,
to bow low in obedience to the ancient rites!'
Exposed and undefended, Inanna replied,
'I have undressed and shown you my identity.
Now where is my older sister?'

The Gatekeeper cringed and retreated
to report to her sister's ancient judges.
The judges interpreted Inanna's confidence and
her celebration of her femininity as arrogance
and hubris and decided she should be punished.
It was her vindictive sister who pointed her finger,
rendering Inanna powerless, before turning her
into a corpse to be hung from a meat hook.

When Southerly Gales Blow

When southerly gales blow,
keening like banshees sharing their
woes, bending boughs to their will
with the noisy intensity of electric drills,
bringing down power lines, damaging
roofs with shrill shrieks of reproof,
this old house creaks and groans
and rocks on its foundation stones.

When grey clouds close in,
wrapping the building like a widow's
shawl and the Fahrenheit falls and
sleet whips the land like pellets of
lead tipping a cat-o'-nine-tails;
despite being forced to sit tight,
sometimes without electric light,
there is something that excites and
thrills whenever Antarctic winds –
like ravenous dingos in search of sheep –
snarl around the neighbouring hills,
and the wails of the wind blow away
complacency or despair and,
leaving onlookers gasping for air,
life slips into overdrive,
reinforcing awareness that being alive
is more than just a heartbeat.

The Great Divide

In the eastern, beachside suburbs,
inner urban culture thrives.
At café tables by the curbs,
latte lovers graze on words.

Sipping chai martinis through
soggy cardboard eco-straws
they can be overheard
discussing important first world concerns

or comparing the performance
of the cars they drive;
the art house movie's perceived flaws;
the dearth of public parking spaces or

providing a precis of the Feminine.
Sharing make-up preserving
air kisses – and the same prejudices –
they are happy provided they are seen.

While, west of the Great Divide,
where skeletal cattle chew dirt for cud,
farmers shoot breeding herds and studs
and worry how they will survive.

Drought

It was summer in the midst of drought.
The earth was parched, impenetrably hard,
and all about leaves fell like rain,
clogging gutters and the drains.
Leaves fell in clouds, curled and dry,
and formed a carpet across the street
that crunched beneath pedestrians' feet
and whenever hot breathed winds eddied by,
blowing veined fragments into the sky,
they blinded eyes like winter sleet.
It was only then, I realised, we were
watching trees trying to survive –
desperately shedding leaves to stay alive.

Love

Love has many permutations; highs and lows.

There is the tender love of a parent for its child.
There is affectionate love between siblings;
love of sport; of an animal pet or *objet d'art*;
devotional love for guru, prophet or messiah.

Love can be a passion igniting sexual
desire and there is also platonic love,
which doesn't seek expression in intimacy.
There are other, not so savoury, variations:
Classical Greece permitted pederasty but

the most important aspect of love appears
to be remaining receptive to its possibility:
to keep love's portal open and, thus, allow love in,
even if having previously experienced love's
woes and the bruises of love's blows.

In a time

In a time of deadly disease,
daily deaths, untold suffering,
plague pits in the USA and the
afflicted boarded up in their houses,
in Wuhan, so they say,
there might be a silver lining,
rampant consumerism is being denied:
cleaner rivers and tides, less polluted air,
animal shelters emptied by human
demand for companionship and despair;
reading Boccaccio's *Decameron* again;
enforced isolation strengthening family ties;
random acts of kindness being recognised.

Covid-19

What's been missed most during
the lockdown associated with Covid-19?
Going to the movies, eating out,
attending live music, the loss of freedom to move about?
Personally, it is having to avoid human contact:
keeping physical distance and social isolation,
touching elbows instead of clasping
a welcoming hand when saying hello to friends;
being reduced to imaginary hugs with
children instead of a loving embrace;
being limited to cyber meetings on Zoom
where 'Mute your microphone please' is a harbinger of doom.
Saddest of all is that some loved ones
are destined to die alone and shunned.

Angelic Beauty

A father but never a parent, I long ago
renounced any right to a relationship with my offspring.
Procreation is simple, paternity complex

and healing sensitivities associated
with renunciation requires tact and toleration
that may or may not be successful.

But I have been blessed: today I heard a
boy-child cry and, holding a grandson
where once was none, gazed in adoration.

No eyes have beheld such angelic beauty!
No thought of the heart so emotionally moving!
The birth of this, or any child, is an epic boon,

proving life is festooned with greater
benefits than self-gratification, the accumulation
of power, pecuniary gain or reputation.

We Were

We were orange and apple,
yin and yang, chalk and cheese
as children; quiet to your loud,
near to your far, circle to your square,
sharing only unruly hair and shelter
from the storm of parental repression
and mutual amusement at our
teenage indiscretions but, now,
more bonded in dying than
in life by a genetic disease,
we share more laughter than depression,
more love than any previous sibling aggression.

Portals

Occasionally, like an unshuttered
window to the night sky, a portal opens;
a portal to an ocean of possibilities;
an invitation to enter other dimensions,
adorned with a myriad of constellations,
unlimited potentialities and, the
possibility, what is called 'love' might enter.

And sometimes love does enter –
sliding down a shaft of starlight
into even hardened hearts and
we leap into a pool of promise
and, in love's bubble, seep like liquid,
together, until, becoming one,
merge like molecules of mercury.

But portals, like all opportunities,
initially need to be perceived
and the enigma of portals is that
we don't know where they lead,
whether transitional or transformational
and, to enter a portal is to surrender,
to let go, to become vulnerable.

And, what if, when wrestling with
the real world, our inner-world
intrudes and, like a home invasion,
the longing for the other becomes
imperative to uplift and sustain and
enmeshment in another's personality
initiates the sublimation of individuality?

And if the beautiful bubble bursts
and the vessel that was replete with
contentment, rapture, pleasure, is emptied,
and all that is left is disappointment,
disillusionment and heartache, does being
bereft mean future portals should be ignored,
like portholes closed to an unsettled sea?

The Cadaver on the Couch

The cadaver on the couch
is my much loved brother.
Once a runner, sportsman,
teacher, friend and lover.
Where did his life force go?
Did it simply disappear
or is his soul somewhere near?
He knew me from embryo
and I keep waiting
for him to say 'hello'.
Where once was activity,
vitality and, sometimes, strife,
now there is no sign of life.
I recognise his profile
but he lies unseeing, immobile,
like a yacht lacking wind
while tendons tighten and
rigor mortis sets in.
Do I detect a smile?
Does he have peace of mind,
I wonder? Like a nut shelled
he lies empty and grim
and what remains is not him.
The cadaver on the couch
was once my brother,
at rest now, no more to suffer.

Only Love

How did they know? How did Christ, John Lennon
and Shams of Tabriz in their, oh, so different ways,
come to comprehend 'love is all there is'?
While millions spend fortunes seeking gurus,
paying fake fakirs, finding avatars, in search of
spiritual truths or, by trying to become pure of heart,
achieve heightened consciousness in the hope
of glimpsing or touching the face of God,
they instinctively knew to ignore the
mirage mystic arts lead to enlightenment:
they knew only love can lead to inner peace.
Was it by owning wounds within their hearts
they learnt only love can salve souls in distress;
that only love can heal and bless a broken spirit;
that only love can provide the igniting spark
for the light that replaces suffering and the dark?

For My Brother

The pulse of the universe is concealed,
like a drop of fresh water inside a sea.
It exists within the breath of living entities;
in the contraction and expansion of a lung
perpetuating that from which life sprung.
Light was first longed for in Stygian darkness,
and, if seeking The Infinite, be guided:
any number can be combined
as many times as it can be divided
and even the finite is undefined.
To ascend, we must first descend:
to feel a presence is to discern its absence.
I held your hand as you died and
felt your soul begin its final glide.

Ozymandias Revisited

What is the difference between rolling
the effigy of a long dead slave trader into a river,
tearing down a statue of Jefferson Davis
in Richmond, once capital of the Confederacy;
defacing Churchill's iconic likeness commemorating
when Britain stood alone against Fascism
and Islamic States' demolition of Palmyra,
once home to Haliphat, or the Taliban destroying
the monumental Buddas of Bamiyan?
Iconoclasm remains the same no matter
the image breakers motive. Will,
like the mutilation of Athens' *hermae*,
the current rage presage ruin and broken
statuary become memorials for yet another age?

Ever Wondered

Ever wondered who you were in a previous life?
Whether it was a life of ease or of strife?
Whether you were a courtesan or faithful wife,
cuckold, soldier, vegetable, wildlife?
Clairvoyants claim there are old souls among us;
those who have been here before and Socrates,
supposedly, said, 'The living spring from the dead,'
that humans rose from the ashes of Titans.

Whether new or old souls, do we return
to learn what we failed to comprehend?
As good ascends and bad descends, does
Karma accumulate through recurring incarnations
until, pure of spirit, we are one with the universe?
If souls do transcend, perhaps it's time to make amends.

The Twisted Ladder

The oncologist said,
'It's a terminal disease,'
effectively informing me
my life is null and void.
And I admit I did pray as
I sat, head bowed, imagining
my DNA, composed
like the holy trinity,
of three separate but
integral parts within
double-stranded helices,
passing through me;
from generations past,
via anti-parallel ladders
of twisting pairs of
molecular strands on
to my distant descendants.

For weeks I lived with that
awful image in my mind;
the DNA helix chirally
revolving in my brain,
imparting genetic instructions
from my mutant genes
to chromosomes inherited
by my only child, grandchildren,
great grandchildren; my
lineage, ad infinitum.

And I reviled and censured
science for being able to
foretell but not prevent
the consequence of that
mutagen active within my cells.
But then came an epiphany
and I understood – the same
science that foretold my fate
might one day, long after listening
to my funeral bells, enable
my progeny to modify their cells.

Charlotte Corday

Brave, brave, Charlotte Corday,
took upon herself to slay
that man of revolutionary
violence, Jean-Paul Marat.

On July thirteenth in ninety-three,
the convent girl from near the sea,
stabbed Marat to death in his bath,
before he could attempt to flee.
Brave, brave Charlotte Corday.

Appalled by all the murdering;
by France's cultural perverting,
Charlotte saved hundreds of thousands
by acting without wavering.
Brave, brave, Charlotte Corday.

Aware her death would be sealed that day,
she killed the journalist who'd betray
Francais by claiming to be 'the people's friend'.
Where oh where are you today?
Brave, brave, Charlotte Corday.

Lockdown

With apologies to *Hamlet* and its author

How could anyone wish not to be
watching a full moon emerge from the sea,
seeing the sun rise over Serengeti savanna
or sinking into the Caribbean, west of Havana
or gaping at the Milky Way, wheeling awesomely
overhead, the night after witnessing a daughter wed.
But in lockdown, alone, it is enough to watch
insects waft their wings and to discern the momentous
in insignificant things. To marvel at willie wagtails
luring threats from their nest, observing a mother and
child at rest; to suddenly see a bird its plumage
had disguised, to feel the omnipotence of the tide.
Humankind may blight but embracing nature
banishes despondency from mind and sight.

To an Aborted Child

The Prophet taught abortion is forbidden –
'haram' – but that, sometimes, there can be
extenuating circumstances which permit the practice.
As a Hindu I believe in 'ahimsa'; the belief any
course of action should be that which causes
least pain to all concerned – but also that a soul
deprived of human existence suffers karmic calamity.
As a Western atheist, the decision is secular,
mine alone, as is any pretence to be emotionally
untouched by the distressing experience.
As a Christian, I stagger beneath the burden of
my guilt and beg forgiveness at St Margaret's feet
but, as a Buddhist in Japan, at the ancient Zojoji Shrine,
I place toys and sweets for you to play with or
taste in the garden of the unborn children,
where I feel your presence and forgiveness…

The Temple

The temple lies in ruins now
desecrated and deserted,
the rituals long forgotten now,
confused, misinterpreted.

This place once resonated with
the singing of ancestral songs,
now none seek divinity's grace,
no congregation throngs.

Sanctified vessels are now pot
sherds and the columns – which
once enclosed this consecrated
space – lie toppled, drums mute

while non-believers efface
or debase engraved holy words.
Now only heaven or the gods
know what is real or shadow.

Here, where traditional hymns were
sung, what was hallowed earth is dust
and people speak in strange tongues.
Here haunted phrases of past prayers

dissolve in the midday glare
and the goddess has long gone –
of her presence there is no trace.
Even fading memories will soon be erased.

Squalls

Here come the squalls,
obscuring and hiding all behind vertical wet walls.

Like shower curtains hung
from low slung clouds, sensuously oscillating

grey shades of spray
cut silent swaths across the breadth of the bay,

akin to gently swaying
dancers in a ballet or kimono-clad geishas

subtly serving a feudal daimyo,
they swivel and swerve until, joining in

a queue with cloud surging
in from the open sea, they swallow the view and

the bay disappears, momentarily
reappears until raindrops carried on the wind

splatter against the window
and, ending visibility, drench everything outside.

Eventually, sated or exhausted,
the squalls begin to subside and, as if swept aside

by an unseen hand, vision clears:
a rainbow rises, reaching skywards, arcs between

distant headlands, joining earth
to patches of blue sky in a rebirth that mystifies.

I Met a Man

I met a man and
he talked at me,
not with me
and, when I
tried to reply,
spoke over me,
rudely, so it
was impossible
to converse.
He did not
speak objectively
and his words
reeked of bigotry,
pretentiousness,
superficiality,
and when he left
I felt depressed
that he was
wandering the world.

Stay a While

Associates of younger days have
now all met their different ends and
I have only memories for friends;
memories embalmed in stone,
friends who no longer answer their phones.
And over there, in the gathering gloom,
stands a stranger in a cowl,
holding an hourglass and scythe,
regarding me with a scowl,
reminding me, no matter
how long ago it began,
all life has an allotted span.
I am alone and dark descends –
and, although I sit by myself,
your presence brings tranquility.
Reader, stay a while with me…
Your empathy is a companion by
my side, your compassion is my guide.

Acknowledgements

The author would like to thank the editors of the literary magazines, periodicals and websites in and on which most of the poems included in this collection were first published or posted:

Social Alternatives (Australia)
Writers Voice (Australia)
Eureka Street (Australia)
Quadrant (Australia)
FreeXpresSion (Australia)
INDaily Adelaide (Australia)
Dyst (Australia)
Milestones anthology, Ginninderra Press (Australia)
Love Lifespan anthology No. 4, Pure Slush (Australia)
Pendle War Poetry Competition anthology (UK)
Erbacce (UK)
Dawntreader (UK,)
War Poetry (UK)
Scrittura (UK)
Untitled Voices (UK)
Sentinel (UK)
Tigershark (UK)
The Ogham Stone (Ireland)
Adelaide Literary Magazine (USA)
Months to Years (USA)
As You Were: Military Experience & the Arts (USA)
The Healing Muse (USA)
Awakened Voices: Those Who Help (USA)
Mahmag Publishing Plague 2020 anthology, (USA)
The Society of Classical Poets (USA)

Grand Little Things (USA)
Poor Yorick (USA)
Scarlet Leaf Review (USA)
Mediterranean Poetry (Sweden)
Anak Sastra (Malaya)
Literature Today No. 7 (India)
Live Encounters (Indonesia)

The poem 'What is commonly called a weed' was a commended entry and subsequently published in the *Red Room Company* & *Royal Botanical Gardens, New Shoots Competition* Anthology (Australia).

'A State Funeral Remembered' was longlisted for the University of Canberra Vice Chancellor's International Poetry Prize 2019 and subsequently published in the competition's anthology, *Silence* (Australia), IPSI: International Poetry Studies Institute, the same year.

The poem 'Inanna and the Gate Keeper' was a finalist for the Adelaide Literary Magazine's 2019 Award Contest (USA) and published in the competition's accompanying anthology in 2020.

www.ingramcontent.com/pod-product-compliance
Lightning Source LLC
Chambersburg PA
CBHW070323120526
44590CB00017B/2801